P9-DVA-674

DISCOVER AMERICA'S NATIONAL PARKS

ABRAHAM LINCOLN

A 19th-century illustration of Abraham Lincoln.

WRITTEN BY TIMOTHY P. TOWNSEND

Copyright 2014 by Eastern National
470 Maryland Drive, Suite 1, Fort Washington, PA 19034
Visit us at www.eParks.com

The America's National Parks Press series is produced by Eastern National, a not-for-profit partner of the National Park Service. Our mission is to promote the public's understanding and support of America's national parks and other public trust partners by providing quality educational experiences, products, and services.

ISBN 978-1-59091-164-8

The following is a look into the life of a very great man, Abraham Lincoln. Today, it is easy to see his greatness. We see Lincoln as the larger-than-life statue in the Lincoln Memorial or the face on Mount Rushmore. We should remember that Lincoln began in very common situations as a farmer, store clerk, attorney, husband, and father. We all agree that he achieved greatness, but we should remember that he did not start out great. Lincoln's life was a demonstration of what he believed—that the United States was established on the basis that no one should have limitations placed upon them.

Abraham Lincoln was born on February 12, 1809, near Hodgenville, Kentucky, the second of three children born to Thomas and Nancy Hanks Lincoln. Lincoln's father was a farmer and carpenter who spent most of his life on the frontier. Lincoln's grandfather was killed by an Indian in Kentucky, leaving his father an orphan at age six. His father "grew up, literally without education," Lincoln wrote many years later. Lincoln's older sister, Sarah, was born in 1807, and his younger brother, Thomas, was born in 1812. Thomas died in infancy.

Lincoln lived with his family on the farm of his birth until 1811, when they moved several miles to a farm on Knob Creek. The Lincoln family stayed on the Knob Creek place another five years until December 1816, when they moved to southern Indiana. Lincoln recorded that the family moved "partly on account of slavery; but chiefly on account of the difficulty in land titles in Ky." Lincoln recalled of his childhood that "I was raised to farm work, which I continued till I was twenty-two."

Tragedy struck young Lincoln when, on October 5, 1818, his mother, Nancy Hanks, died of milk sickness, an ailment that occurs when the milk from a cow that had eaten the white snakeroot plant is consumed.

Left: Painting of Abraham Lincoln by George Peter Alexander.

The death of Lincoln's mother left young Lincoln and his sister, Sarah, responsible for the great amount of work involved with maintaining a frontier home and farm.

The following year, Thomas Lincoln left the two children at their Indiana farm and traveled to Elizabethtown, Kentucky, where he married widow Sarah Bush Johnston. Thomas then returned home to his children with his new wife and her three children. Lincoln recalled that Sarah "proved a good and kind mother." As the years went by, the new Lincoln family continued to farm, and the children attended school when they could. Lincoln later recounted that he "went to A.B.C. schools by littles," and the aggregate of all his schooling did not amount to one year. He always regretted his lack of formal schooling but looked for opportunities for more education, writing that he "regrets his want of education, and does what he can to supply the want."

Tragedy again befell the Lincolns when Lincoln's sister, Sarah, died while in childbirth in January 1828. Lincoln experienced the death of his mother and sister within 10 years of one another on the harsh frontier.

In 1830, the Lincoln family was again on the move, this time to Illinois. In March, they settled along the Sangamon River, 10 miles southwest of Decatur. The following year, Lincoln set out on his own for the first time and settled in New Salem, Illinois.

Within a year of Lincoln's arrival at New Salem, he began his political career by entering the race for the Illinois legislature. His campaign was interrupted when he joined other volunteers in forming an Illinois militia unit at the beginning of the

Abraham Lincoln reading by firelight with his stepmother, Sarah Bush Johnston Lincoln.

Black Hawk War. The company elected Lincoln as their captain, and Lincoln later recalled that "he has not since had any success in life which gave him so much satisfaction." Lincoln traveled throughout northern Illinois during his four-month service in the Black Hawk War and later joked that in his military service, he had "a good many bloody struggles with the musquetoes."

This print, Lincoln the Rail Splitter, *ca. 1909, depicts Lincoln splitting logs to make rail fences.*

Lincoln held a variety of jobs during his time in New Salem. In 1833, he invested in a New Salem store and later in the year, was appointed postmaster. In 1834, he took up land surveying and won his first election to public office as a representative in the Illinois legislature. Lincoln took his legislative seat in the state capitol at Vandalia and was reelected in 1836. It was during this time that fellow legislator John Todd Stuart persuaded Lincoln to study law.

In February 1837, the Illinois legislature approved the transfer of the Illinois capital from Vandalia to Springfield. Lincoln concluded that his prospects were much brighter in the newly designated capital city, and in April 1837, he moved to Springfield to begin practicing law as a junior partner with Stuart. Lincoln didn't arrive with very much but was befriended by Springfield merchant Joshua Speed, who offered to share his room above his general store with Lincoln, and the two developed a lifelong friendship.

This is the earliest-known photograph of Lincoln. It is a daguerreotype, ca. 1848.

During this time, Lincoln began courting Mary Ann Todd. Mary was visiting from her home in Lexington, Kentucky, and was staying with her sister, Elizabeth Todd Edwards. Lincoln and Mary were wed on November 4, 1842, at the home of Elizabeth and Ninian Edwards. Lincoln later corresponded to a friend, saying, "Nothing new here, except my marrying, which to me, is matter of profound wonder." The newlyweds moved into a rooming house known as the Globe Tavern in downtown Springfield, which is where their first son, Robert Todd Lincoln, was born on August 1, 1843. On May 1, 1844, the Lincoln family moved into the home they would live in for the next 17 years, at the corner of Eighth and Jackson Streets. Two years later, on March 10, 1846, the couple's second son, Edward Baker Lincoln, was born.

With a growing family to support, Lincoln continued his legal career, traveling extensively throughout central Illinois on the Eighth Judicial Circuit. As a circuit-riding attorney, Lincoln was better able to make a name for himself as an attorney and politician. Lincoln and Stuart dissolved their law partnership in April 1841, and Lincoln formed a new firm with Stephen T. Logan. The firm of Logan and Lincoln continued until 1844, when Lincoln became the senior partner of the law firm of Lincoln and Herndon with William H. Herndon.

In 1846, Lincoln was elected as a representative in the Thirtieth U.S. Congress. The following year, he brought his family with him to Washington for the beginning of his term. Mary and the boys eventually left Washington, in part because Lincoln thought Mary "hindered me some in attending to business." A few months later, however, Lincoln wrote that "having nothing but business—no variety" made life "exceedingly tasteless."

A Self-Made Man

Few American presidents received a more meager education than Abraham Lincoln. Yet none have written or spoken with greater eloquence. In his own words, he grew up in a "wild region" where "there was absolutely nothing to excite ambition for education." Lincoln's schooling consisted of no more than a year's worth of classes taught by a series of visiting teachers. But demonstrating the determination so much a part of the 19th-century ideal of the self-made man, Lincoln responded to "the pressure of necessity" and set about educating himself. He read voraciously, borrowing books from whomever he could and often rereading volumes when he could locate nothing new. He numbered the King James Bible, Aesop's Fables, Bunyan's Pilgrim's Progress, Defoe's Robinson Crusoe, Shakespeare's plays, and Franklin's autobiography among his favorites.

Lincoln's drive for self-education outlasted his youth. Unable to pay for law school, he borrowed law books and, in his own words, "studied with nobody." As a circuit-riding lawyer in the 1830s, he mastered six volumes of Euclidean geometry in order to sharpen his powers of logic and language. In an 1859 speech, Lincoln saluted the importance of reading, which "gives access to whatever has already been discovered by others." Today we might label the 16th president a "lifelong learner."

Lincoln, in his boyhood, reading by firelight, lithograph, ca. 1868.

On February 1, 1850, the Lincoln family suffered a great loss when three-year-old Eddie Lincoln died of what was called "consumption," probably tuberculosis. A funeral service was held in the Lincolns' parlor the following day, and several days later, a poetic tribute titled "Little Eddie" appeared in the *Illinois Daily Journal*. Later that month, Lincoln updated his stepbrother, John Johnston, about the loss. "I suppose you had not learned that we lost our little boy. We miss him very much." The sadness at the loss of Eddie must have been lessened somewhat with the arrival of Lincoln's third son, William Wallace, on December 21, 1850. The family greeted their fourth son, Thomas, or "Tad" as he was called, on April 4, 1853. The family was complete with the addition of Fido, the dog.

With the end of his term in the U.S. Congress, Lincoln focused on his law practice until he learned about the passage of the Kansas-Nebraska Act of 1854. This law, championed by Illinois Senator Stephen A. Douglas, let the people of the western territories decide for themselves if their territory should become a free or slave state. Lincoln saw this and the Supreme Court's *Dred Scott* decision, which ruled that blacks could not be U.S. citizens, as steps toward nationalization of slavery. Lincoln was always opposed to slavery, but he also believed that slavery was protected by the U.S. Constitution. He was convinced that if slavery was contained, it would end on its own. The Kansas-Nebraska Act allowed for slavery's unlimited expansion. Lincoln felt compelled to act to change that law.

In 1854, Lincoln attempted to put himself in a position where he could affect real change to the Kansas-Nebraska Act. He eyed a seat in the Illinois legislature as well as the U.S. Senate but did not end up with either office. He then looked to 1858, and the U.S. Senate seat held by Douglas. On June 16, 1858, Lincoln kicked off his efforts against Douglas by giving his "House Divided" speech in the Illinois statehouse, telling those in attendance that "A house divided against itself cannot stand. I believe this government cannot endure, permanently half slave and half free."

In the summer and fall of 1858, Lincoln engaged in a series of debates with Douglas that included stops at seven communities across Illinois and grabbed the nation's attention. The debates focused almost exclusively on

Left: Depiction of one of the Lincoln-Douglas debates of 1858.

The Short and Simple Annals of the Poor

When asked to sum up his youth in 1860, Abraham Lincoln told campaign biographer J. L. Scripps, "My early history is perfectly characterized by a single line of Thomas Gray's Elegy: 'The short and simple annals of the poor.'" Reared in poverty in Kentucky and Indiana, the young Lincoln developed a lifelong distaste for farm labor. After his father, Thomas, lost all of his considerable land holdings in Kentucky, the family moved to Indiana. There, the nine-year-old Lincoln lost his mother to illness. His father soon married a woman with whom Lincoln developed a close and loving relationship.

Lincoln proved to be a dutiful son, sharing the workload with his father, but at the same time becoming increasingly alienated from him due to Thomas' lack of education and failure to appreciate his son's ambition. When he was 19, Lincoln made his first break from home, ferrying a flatboat load of goods down the Mississippi River to be sold in New Orleans. In 1832, Lincoln left his family's new homestead in Illinois for good, settling in the small town of New Salem. Although he maintained a relationship with his stepmother, Sarah, Lincoln saw his father very rarely during the remaining 20 years of Thomas' life.

Nineteen-year-old Abraham Lincoln as a flatboatman on the Mississippi River.

An American flag banner promoting Lincoln as the 1860 Republican Party candidate for president.

the expansion of slavery into the western territories. Lincoln did well in the debates but lost the Senate race, writing later that "I believe I have made some marks which will tell for the cause of liberty long after I am gone."

Lincoln did not give up. He spent the next two years giving speeches throughout the country. These efforts gained him the attention of Republican Party leaders who were considering him for an 1860 run for the presidency. One of the most important speeches Lincoln made was at New York's Cooper Institute on the evening of February 27, 1860. Lincoln argued that the nation's founders did not want slavery to expand in the nation. He quickly won the admiration of the audience, and a *New York Tribune* reporter wrote, "No man ever before made such an impression on his first appeal to a New York audience."

Before leaving New York, Lincoln took the time to visit the notorious Five Points area in Manhattan. Five Points was the center of poverty, crime, and disease and one of the few areas where the city's immigrants, mainly Irish and German, as well as African Americans, could afford to live.

Lincoln arriving for his inauguration as 16th president of the United States on March 4, 1861.

Lincoln went into the "Five Points House of Industry," a facility for children in the area, and told them about the challenges he faced as a child growing up on the frontier. When he was thanked for the way he inspired the children, he replied, "No, they are the ones who have inspired me—given me courage.... I am glad we came—I shall never forget this as long as I live."

On May 18, 1860, Lincoln was chosen as the Republican nominee for the presidency at the Republican National Convention in Chicago. From the time of his nomination, Lincoln's schedule was constantly filled with the requests, demands, or urgings of others. But Lincoln still found time to write a letter of encouragement to young George Latham, who, Lincoln learned from his son, Robert, had failed the Harvard entrance exams. "Again I say let no feeling of discouragement prey upon you, and in the end you are sure to succeed."

Lincoln spent all of Election Day, November 6, 1860, monitoring the election results. At about 1:30 am the following morning, Lincoln proceeded home announcing, "Mary, Mary, we are elected!" But, a dark cloud hung over the election since Lincoln's name did not appear on most Southern ballots because many voters in the Southern states believed that Lincoln would end slavery if elected. Lincoln received only 40 percent of the popular vote to Northern Democrat Stephen A. Douglas' 29 percent, Southern Democrat John C. Breckinridge's 18 percent, and Constitutional Union John Bell's 13 percent.

Within a month of his election, Lincoln traveled to Chicago to meet Vice President Hannibal Hamlin of Maine. He also visited an area of Chicago called "The Sands," one of the worst areas of Chicago for crime and poverty. Lincoln spoke to children at a facility called the "North Market Hall Mission," telling them, "with close attention to your teachers, and hard work to put into practice what you learn from them, some one of you may also become president of the United States in due time like myself."

Lincoln took time at the end of January 1861, just prior to his departure for Washington, to travel to Coles County, Illinois, to see his stepmother and visit his father's grave. In the midst of the last-minute details for a move to the White House, word reached Springfield that on February 4, 1861, Southern states that had left the nation because of Lincoln's election had formed the Confederate States of America. On February 11, 1861, Lincoln hinted at the difficult job ahead of him in his farewell address to the people of Springfield at the Great Western Railroad Depot when he said

Abraham and Mary

On November 4, 1842, Abraham Lincoln wed a woman far more socially skilled and well-educated than he. Born into a wealthy Lexington family, Mary Todd had received a first-rate education before moving to Springfield in 1839. There, she met Lincoln, whose interests in politics she shared. Their courtship, fraught with uncertainty, featured a broken engagement and ultimate reconciliation.

The first of their four sons—Robert—was born nine months after the wedding; Edward arrived in 1846; Willie in 1850; and Tad in 1853. Because

Lincoln's thriving legal practice took him away from Springfield for months at a time, Mary had primary responsibility for managing the family's domestic affairs. The Lincolns had to endure the premature deaths of Eddie in 1850 and Willie in 1862.

Lincoln's frequent bouts of melancholy combined with Mary's temper and mood swings to create a combustible marital relationship that only grew more so amid the pressures of life in the White House. The president's assassination and Tad's death in 1871 devastated Mary, and she suffered the additional trauma of being committed for a short time to a mental asylum. She died in 1882. Robert died in 1926, after a long career combining public service with business success.

The Lincoln family, after a painting by Francis B. Carpenter, 1861.

President Lincoln and his cabinet adopting the Emancipation Proclamation, lithograph by Currier & Ives, 1876.

that in his presidency was "a task before me greater than that which rested upon Washington."

On March 4, 1861, Lincoln was inaugurated as the 16th president of the United States. Even during this time of crisis with civil war on the horizon, Lincoln held out the hope for peace in his inaugural address. "We are not enemies, but friends. We must not be enemies." This last-minute appeal failed to stop the approaching war. On April 12, 1861, Fort Sumter in Charleston Harbor, South Carolina, was fired upon by Southern forces. The "House Divided" crisis that Lincoln had predicted two years earlier had come to pass. The Confederate States of America included South Carolina, Georgia, Florida, Alabama, Mississippi, Texas, Louisiana, Virginia, Arkansas, Tennessee, and North Carolina. Lincoln's presidency proved to be the most difficult in history, with a term in office dominated by bloody civil war that cost the nation an estimated 750,000 lives.

Even though the war demanded much of Lincoln's time, he made sure that he saw his children. His oldest son, Robert, regularly visited from Harvard, and Willie and Tad were allowed to interrupt meetings whenever they liked. The Lincoln family felt the tragedy of the Civil War in many ways but was especially struck when, on February 20, 1862, their son, Willie, died, probably of typhoid fever. Despite the loss of his son, Lincoln had to continue to direct the war and the country.

Slavery was the divisive issue that helped propel Lincoln to the White House and thrust the nation into civil war. Lincoln maintained that as president he could not end slavery. But by the summer of 1862, with the war raging on, Lincoln had drafted an Emancipation Proclamation after concluding that as commander in chief of the armed forces, it was legal for him to free the slaves as a necessary war measure. Lincoln called his cabinet together on July 22 and read the Emancipation Proclamation to them. They suggested that Lincoln should wait for a Union victory so the proclamation did not seem to be a desperate move by a losing army.

Later that year, on September 17, 1862, the bloodiest single day of the Civil War, Union General George B. McClellan met Robert E. Lee's Confederate forces at Antietam Creek near Sharpsburg, Maryland, and drove Lee back into Virginia. This was the victory that Lincoln was waiting for, and on September 22, he issued the preliminary Emancipation Proclamation. The final proclamation was signed and took effect on January 1, 1863.

On November 2, 1863, Lincoln received an invitation to give a speech at the dedication of a military cemetery at Gettysburg, Pennsylvania, to honor those who died at the July 1-3, 1863 battle. At Gettysburg, 51,000 soldiers were killed, wounded, or captured, making it the bloodiest battle of the Civil War. On November 19, 1863, following a two-hour speech from the featured speaker, Edward Everett, Lincoln rose and gave his brief Gettysburg Address in which he told the audience that the United States was a nation "conceived in liberty, and dedicated to the proposition that all men are created equal." He then called for "a new birth of freedom."

Because of the war, Lincoln was constantly reminded of death. When

Lincoln delivering his Gettysburg Address on November 19, 1863, lithograph, 1905.

he learned that an Illinois friend had been killed in battle, he wrote a letter to the friend's daughter, Fanny McCullough. "Sorrow comes to all," he wrote, "and, to the young, it comes with bitterest agony. The memory of your dear Father will yet be a sad sweet feeling in your heart."

Lincoln protected life whenever he could. His compassion for soldiers condemned to death for desertion, falling asleep at their post, and other minor offenses is well known. In 1863, Lincoln's secretary, John Hay, wrote about Lincoln's aversion to executions in his diary: "Cases of cowardice he was specially averse to punishing with death. He said it would frighten the poor devils too terribly, to shoot them."

Despite the stress and sacrifice of the office, Lincoln was interested in retaining the presidency for another term and ran for reelection in 1864. Lincoln's opponent in the election was General McClellan. McClellan did not feel that ending slavery was important, and his party concluded that the war was a failure. McClellan's popularity also came at a time when Lincoln's support was faltering. Newspapers were critical of the cost of the war and accused Lincoln of not caring about the loss of life and the nation's

President Lincoln is greeted by Union soldiers and freedmen in Virginia, March 1865.

dire situation. By August 1864, Lincoln's political insiders advised him that his reelection was in jeopardy. One Republican leader wrote, "I have told Mr. Lincoln that his re-election was an impossibility."

Several events helped to turn the tide for Lincoln and his quest to retain the presidency; one of the most important was General Sherman's military capture of Atlanta. The results of the election brought Abraham Lincoln

The Gettysburg Address

On November 19, 1863, Abraham Lincoln used a mere 272 words when rendering one of the most profound speeches in American history. Invited to deliver "a few appropriate remarks" at the consecration of the national cemetery in Gettysburg, Pennsylvania, the president's address followed a long oration by Edward Everett, a former member of the House and Senate, governor of Massachusetts, secretary of state, minister to Great Britain, and Harvard president.

Contrary to a popular myth, Lincoln did not jot down his remarks on the back of an envelope while traveling by train to Gettysburg. Rather, he worked hard on a speech that in a few paragraphs reminded listeners of the promise of the Declaration of Independence, rededicated the Civil War to the Union's preservation, honored the fallen Union soldiers, and forecasted "a new birth of freedom."

The public response to the address divided along partisan lines, but the speaker who shared the platform with Lincoln wrote that he "should be glad" if he had come "as near to the central idea of the occasion, in two hours, as you did in two minutes." Today, five copies of the Gettysburg Address exist, all differing in minor respects and all grist for scholars' close readings of one of our nation's greatest public utterances.

This photograph by Alexander Gardner was taken on November 8, 1863, 11 days before Lincoln delivered the Gettysburg Address.

The assassination of President Abraham Lincoln by John Wilkes Booth, lithograph, 1865, by Currier & Ives.

55 percent of the popular vote to George B. McClellan's 45 percent. By the time Lincoln gave his second inaugural address on March 4, 1865, Union victory was all but assured, and Lincoln used the inaugural address to remind all that the war was fought over slavery. "These slaves constituted a peculiar and powerful interest. All knew that this interest was, somehow, the cause of the war." But he also used this moment to begin to reunite the nation by saying the country should act "With malice toward none; with charity for all."

Now that Lincoln had guided the country through the Civil War, he began to concentrate on repairing the nation and life with his family. On April 14, 1865, he and Mary took a carriage ride and talked of their son, Willie, who had died three years earlier. They talked of their plans for the future when they could perhaps travel and return to the quiet of their Springfield home. Mary recalled that Lincoln seemed more cheerful than he had been in a long time.

Later that evening, Abraham and Mary attended a play at Ford's Theatre, and at 10:30 pm, Confederate sympathizer John Wilkes Booth entered the presidential theater box, put a derringer pistol to the back of Lincoln's head, and fired. Lincoln was taken to the Petersen House, across the street from the theater, where he died at 7:22 am the following day. On April 21, after funeral services in the White House, the Lincoln funeral train, with Lincoln's remains and those of his son, Willie, departed Washington and began a 12-day trip back to Springfield, reversing Lincoln's 1861 inaugural route, to bring him home.

The American people responded to Lincoln's death with a variety of gestures to express their feelings of grief. Throughout the nation, eulogies were given, poems and songs were written, artwork was produced, and cities located along the funeral train route were draped in black. The funeral train arrived in Springfield on May 3, and Lincoln's remains were placed in representative's hall of the statehouse, where he had given his "House Divided" speech seven years earlier. At 11:30 am the following day, the Lincoln funeral procession, led by Lincoln's horse, "Old Bob," left the statehouse and passed buildings associated with Lincoln's life on its way to Oak Ridge Cemetery, where Lincoln's remains, along with the remains of Willie, were laid to rest.

Lincoln had come a long way from the time of his birth in Kentucky. That frontier boy influenced a great many people and events, and we still live in his shadow. We try to understand him, both where he came from and how he was able to achieve what he did. We attempt this by studying his life through the many books that have been written and by visiting historic sites and museums dedicated to commemorating his life. Historic sites, libraries, and museums that honor Abraham Lincoln are located throughout the nation and are visited by millions of people every year. We visit those places to become inspired, not so much by a president but by an average man who was able to achieve great things. We know that, because of the leadership of Lincoln and the efforts of many others, the same possibilities are available to any of us today. As Lincoln said, "some one of you may also become president of the United States in due time like myself."

The Emancipation Proclamation

On January 1, 1863, Abraham Lincoln signed the Emancipation Proclamation and instantly transformed the American Civil War into a conflict to abolish slavery. The proclamation did

Emancipation Proclamation, *painting by A.A. Lamb, 1863.*

not outlaw slavery completely or make the new freedmen citizens. It freed slaves only in the 10 states still in rebellion and ignored those in the border states of Maryland, Delaware, Kentucky, and Missouri. It also exempted Tennessee, the new state of West Virginia, and parts of Louisiana and the Tidewater region of Virginia. The proclamation immediately liberated no more than 50,000 slaves already behind Union lines, but that

number grew dramatically as Union troops advanced deeper into the Confederacy.

Later generations have praised Lincoln's action, which he based on his authority as the nation's commander in chief, but many of his contemporaries opposed the proclamation. Southern slaveholders resisted the seizure of capital assets worth more than $3 billion, and racial prejudice drove many whites in the North to criticize the president. For some abolitionists, it was too timid an act. But most African American leaders agreed with Frederick Douglass that the proclamation represented "the answer to the agonizing prayers of centuries." The ratification of the Thirteenth Amendment to the Constitution three years later assured the end of slavery throughout the United States.

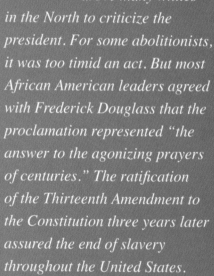

Right: Abraham Lincoln, 16th president of the United States, color engraving, ca. 1865.

The following National Park Service sites interpret different aspects of Abraham Lincoln's life. For more information on our national parks, please visit www.nps.gov.

Abraham Lincoln Birthplace National Historical Park

Lincoln was born in a single room log cabin near Hodgenville, Kentucky, on Sunday, February 12, 1809. His early years on the Kentucky frontier helped shape his character. The country's first memorial to Lincoln enshrines the symbolic birthplace cabin.

Lincoln Boyhood National Memorial in Lincoln City, Indiana, preserves the site of the farm where Abraham Lincoln spent 14 formative years of his life, from the ages of 7 to 21. He and his family moved to Indiana in 1816 and stayed until 1830, when they moved to Illinois. During this period, Lincoln grew physically and intellectually into a man.

Lincoln Home National Historic Site preserves the home in Springfield, Illinois, where Lincoln lived for 17 years before he became president. The surrounding historic district preserves the 1860s environment in which the Lincoln family lived. Here, we see Lincoln as a spouse, parent, and neighbor.

Ford's Theatre National Historic Site in Washington, D.C., preserves the theater where President Lincoln was shot on April 14, 1865. He was carried across the street to the Petersen House, where he died the next morning. The park examines the motivation behind Lincoln's assassination.

The Lincoln Memorial in Washington, D.C., was built to continue Lincoln's legacy. Daniel Chester French designed the Lincoln statue to be the focal point of the memorial. Marble and limestone from both the North and South were chosen to construct the memorial to continue Lincoln's vision for a unified nation.

Mount Rushmore National Memorial began as an idea to attract visitors to South Dakota in the 1920s. Gutzon Borglum carved George Washington, Thomas Jefferson, Theodore Roosevelt, and Abraham Lincoln into a "Shrine of Democracy." These men played important roles in the development of the United States.

Mount Rushmore